MW00652684

First published 2012 by Brechin Books Limited

6 Brechin Place, London SW7 4QA

Copyright © Warren Lamb and Eden Davies
2012

ISBN 978-0-9540284-3-5

Typeset in Calibri

Designed & Printed in England.

The Authors reserve the moral right to be
identified as the authors of this work in
accordance with the copyright Design and
Patents Act 1988

All rights reserved. No part of this publication
may be reproduced, stored in a retrieval
system, or transmitted in any form or by any
means, electronic, photocopying, recording or
otherwise without the prior permission of the
publishers.

A FRAMEWORK FOR UNDERSTANDING MOVEMENT

...my *Seven* Creative Concepts...

By Warren Lamb

in collaboration with **Eden Davies**

Drawings by **Steve Hurst**

Cover & design by **Perception Graphics**

i

CONTENTS

ILLUSTRATIONS

Warren Lamb

ABOUT THE AUTHOR

Warren Lamb was born in Wallasey, Merseyside, in northern England in 1923. He was educated at Wallasey Grammar School but left at 16 to join Lloyds Bank. In February 1941, as soon as he was old enough, he joined the Royal Navy and saw active service in World War II after which he reluctantly returned to banking.

As a young man he had an interest in the theatre and amateur dramatics (though not specifically in being an actor) and this led him in 1946 to attend a lecture on Rudolf Laban, the man who would become his inspiration and mentor. Laban, a choreographer and leading pioneer of modern dance, had come to England as a refugee in 1938 and by 1946 was becoming well-known in Britain as a teacher of dance and movement.[1] Shortly after this introduction, and to his parents' great concern, Warren abandoned banking and enrolled at the Art of Movement Studio in Manchester run by Lisa Ullmann. Laban immediately appreciated that here was a student with a natural understanding of movement, and with a particular ability to grasp the principles of Effort. During the war years Laban had built up a close association with one of England's first management consultants, F C Lawrence at Paton, Lawrence and Co. He introduced Warren Lamb to Lawrence and, while still a student of movement and dance, Warren was engaged in making Effort notations in some of Lawrence's client companies, as well as teaching Effort to fellow students.

After his three years at the Art of Movement Studio, Warren continued to work with Lawrence and Laban for more than ten years, first as an apprentice, and later as a colleague. Whilst contemporaries at the Art of Movement Studio became teachers, dancers and choreographers, his path was set at this early stage into the application of movement study in the everyday world. Initially for Paton, Lawrence & Co. he was required simply to make Effort notations of operatives at work, but as this revealed the difference in the way one person worked in comparison with another at the same task, it moved naturally into using notation to assess the right worker for a particular part of the production process, and eventually into selection for more senior appointments. His notation, analysis and his recommendations had to be explained to the accountants and engineers employed by Paton Lawrence & Co, and it was this discipline which challenged him to find a framework which would encompass the theory of movement in a meaningful way without losing the true sense that movement is a constant process of variation.

During this time he used the categories of movement taught to him by Laban, Functional Action, Shadow Movement and Body Attitude. As the analysis work became more sophisticated these categories became inadequate, and gradually after Laban's death in 1958 Warren Lamb's Seven Creative Concepts emerged from the profusion of ideas and theory of movement that was Laban's legacy. As the person who worked most closely with Laban during his last few years, Warren was sought out by numerous people anxious to learn more about him, among them psychiatrist Judith Kestenberg, Laban student Irmgard Bartenieff, and Laban's daughter Juana. The process of teaching and exchanging ideas with them in turn helped to clarify Warren's emerging theories.

In 1952 Warren Lamb left Paton, Lawrence & Co to set up his own company, Warren Lamb Associates. Throughout his subsequent career he has been retained by an impressive list of major companies, some of which stayed with him for decades, seeking his advice on the selection and training of their management teams. In those early days he described his work as Aptitude Assessment. This was later changed to Action Profiling by Pamela Ramsden who joined him in 1970. She devised training courses and developed the basis of their work which was by now almost exclusively with senior management. In 1982 Pamela Ramsden set up her own organisation but they continued to be in contact until a difference of interpretation caused a split in 1992. As a result Warren Lamb left Action Profilers International and since then has worked with a small professional group under the banner of Movement Pattern Analysis.

Throughout his long career Warren Lamb has been eager that the study of movement should be regarded as a subject in its own right. He has fought often at cost to his own career, to protect his theories from plagiarism or over-simplification. His belief is that the study of movement, since it is part of every activity, should be applied in a multi-disciplinary fashion and because of this he has worked with a wide variety of people: sculptors, artists, musicians, actors, teachers, therapists and psychiatrists. Whilst most of his work has been in industrial and commercial fields he has nonetheless remained closely involved with his colleagues from the Art of Movement Studio, and with other activities of the Laban Guild.

"Lamb has arrived at a form of theory that has been informed by practice. Rather than engaging in purely theoretical speculation about movement or confining his transmission to 'on the job' training, he has constantly tested the one against the other – a theory of movement that moves in the process of its elaboration. Lamb hasn't always worked in the spirit of Laban, because that isn't part of his own pattern – they really are two very different men. What we are left with is a body of work that is still being refined and which has added immeasurably to our understanding of the meaning and value of movement." (McCaw, 2006. p.212)

Warren Lamb has now retired from active consultancy but is continuously engaged in training and lecturing on movement. He lives in London and Los Angeles.

EDEN DAVIES *November 2011*

Endnotes

*(1) A short biography of Laban and Warren Lamb's early career with him can be found in **Beyond Dance**. There are many good biographies of Laban available.*

...my *Seven* Creative Concepts...

By Warren Lamb

INTRODUCTION

The Seven Creative Concepts were formulated in the years immediately following Laban's death in 1958, when I was focusing on finding a workable framework incorporating everything I had learnt during my apprenticeship with him. The concepts were not published until the early 1980s when they were set out in the newsletter *Action News*, then the quarterly publication of Warren Lamb Associates.

This was edited by Carol-Lynne Moore, now Director of training for Movement Pattern Analysis, and a leader in the field of movement study. Carol-Lynne had asked me to tell the story of the development of Movement Pattern Analysis (at that time called Action Profiling) and to this end I contributed four instalments for *Action News*. It was in the fourth of these instalments that I defined the concepts for which I had been solely responsible and which I had developed in those years subsequent to Laban's death. This was the first time they appeared as the basis for what was to become Movement Pattern Analysis. Somewhere along the line they have been dubbed "Creative Concepts".

Since then they have acquired a life of their own. For example, a three day seminar in Minneapolis in 2007 promoted by the professional institute *Motus Humanus* concentrated on the concepts and they were seen by the forty participants as having significance beyond the techniques of Movement Pattern Analysis. All seven concepts have been extensively applied to every field of movement study including dance, education, therapy and the arts. This being so, it is inevitable that at times they have become diffused, incorrectly defined or distorted by practitioners unclear as to their origin and adapting them for their own particular purposes. I have therefore been encouraged to write this booklet by Eden Davies, (author of *Beyond Dance*), to offer correction and clarification, and to set down for all time the origins of the Seven Creative Concepts. Hopefully, after this my responsibility for them will remain recognised, the concepts will be better understood, and distortion will be discouraged.

I will concentrate only on the Seven Concepts as they are applied in the field of Movement Pattern Analysis and related fields. Because Laban had such a broad range of influence they, or some version of them, have spread far and wide, which is to be expected because the study of movement is open to anyone and not just those involved in the obvious fields. I have met people from all walks of life with a natural ability to observe movement, many of them from fields altogether unrelated to movement study. I have also met many highly qualified in some aspect of physical activity who have difficulty in recognising how movement can be studied. Sports trainers, martial arts people and dancers all have their particular way of analysing what they are doing and how to do it better, but this does not mean they will automatically understand the content of the movement they are watching.

For example, a movement may be quick but to what degree is it accelerating and decelerating? A movement may look strong but have we seen the process of the pressure increasing and decreasing? We may see a person directing their gaze at another person but do we see the process – or rhythm – of relative directing to indirecting? The answer is that the majority of people do not see the processes which constitute movement, and consequently they have a problem with understanding movement observation. **A natural ability to do so is what I call a heightened *kinaesthetic sense*, and this is essential to movement observation.**

There is movement going on in the body constantly although much of it is too small to be observed by the human eye. Laban talked about movement as a perpetual state of flux, and out of this flux we are constantly selecting, in our own behaviour or for observation, certain movement processes more than others. If as observers we record only fixed positions it is like taking one note from a piece of music and trying to give it meaning. Laban recognised this; although he enabled a disciplined study of movement by means of the notation he developed, he is quoted as saying he regretted agreeing to what is now known as Labanotation because it is based on a point to point method of description instead of on continuity of movement. Dr Jeffrey Longstaff has written an excellent paper on this, *Continuous Flux in Flow of Effort and Shape,* which appeared in *Movement and Dance* in 2008.

Laban's compromise in developing a method of notation was probably necessary for him to reach the dance public he was then seeking, but my experience of working closely with him for twelve years is unequivocal. For him movement had no points – it was a constant state of flux. Labanotation is valuable to choreographers because it offers tools for creating a record of their work analogous to the score of a music composition, but as Laban became increasingly absorbed with the expressivity of dance, so had the notation to become more subtle. As movement analysis developed the notation developed for dance had to go through yet more changes to accurately describe the constancy of flux in movement rather than just its spatial orientation from point to point. The observer now needed to record each component relative to other components in movement sequences, in which only one interpretation was possible as to what was happening between each symbol. It had to be seen precisely both as one process of variation, and as describing a state of flux.

Similarly, the terminology has been developed from the terms originally used by Laban. For example, to maintain an awareness of a constant process of variation I have introduced present participles of verbs such as Freeing and Binding where Laban had used 'Free' and 'Bound' as descriptions of the range of Flow of Effort. The important fact remains however: the changes made to enhance the interpretation of movement in all its subtleties in no way change the essential theoretical basis on which movement analysis stands.

Carol-Lynne Moore has developed a training programme which trains people to observe and record movement but a heightened kinaesthetic sense is still a prerequisite and, even so, it needs a lot of hard work and practice to become a movement observer. In the introductory papers for a recent course on Movement Pattern Analysis she wrote:

"Movement is everywhere, in the heavens, on earth, in the daily course of human action and interaction. Of all these ceaseless motions, the ones that matter most are human. And this is not surprising, for movement is an omnipresent accompaniment to human endeavours of all kinds."

She goes on to make important points about recent developments. There is now clear evidence that most movement – human movement – elicits a sympathetic reaction in the brain. This reaction is caused by what are called 'mirror neurons' which, as their title suggests, create an internal mirroring, or representation, of the movement which we observe in others. This prompts her to declare that "we are all people watchers".

We all observe movement and form impressions of people from what we see, usually subconsciously. But to progress beyond simple impressions there had first to be both a notation system and a language in which it could be discussed. Laban started this by describing movement in terms of its various component parts. He put these into two groups, Eukinetics (Effort) and Choreutics (Shape), and subdivided these into three Effort elements and three ranges of Shape, from which all the intricacies of his "Effort Rhythm" and "Space Harmonies" derive. After his death it was for me to complete the process by building on the concepts he had given us and organising his wide-ranging theories into a purposeful framework. This process resulted in the Seven Creative Concepts, which together enable a meaningful interpretation of human movement. In 1979 Elizabeth Watson and I published the aptly titled *Body Code,* the first chapter of which is called *The Secret Language.*

The step from observing to understanding human movement required finding the tools which in a sense break the code of this silent language.

The Seven Creative Concepts are here presented in a logical order connected to the order in which they were formulated. The student reading them for the first time might therefore find it necessary to digest each Concept in turn before proceeding to the next, because each subsequent Concept assumes a familiarity with the basic tenets set out earlier. These basic tenets, the Decision-Making Process, the Posture-Gesture Merger, and the Effort/Shape Framework form the cornerstones of Movement Pattern Analysis.

CONCEPT ONE

The concept of a Decision-Making sequence enabling emphasis to be put on the Process as distinct from the content of a decision.

We all take decisions constantly throughout the day. Some will be small, "What colour socks will I wear today?", and some will be life-changing, "Should I apply for that job I saw advertised?", or "Should I propose to my girl/boy-friend?". Each person has their preferred manner of arriving at decisions and will apply this preferred manner to questions large or small when circumstances permit them to do so. This has nothing to do with whether their decision in each case will be a good one or a bad one, but being able to arrive at the decision in the way we prefer is fundamental to our well-being and will in fact enhance the chances of it being a good decision.

Pressures, for example of time, environment or authority, will often make it difficult for us to exercise our preferred way of taking decisions. Everyone suffers this to some extent, typically if they are in an unsuitable job or a difficult work environment, or if they are in a relationship where they are put under a lot of pressure. A person who lives in such a situation will inevitably have constraints on their choices in life; they will experience some form of stress and make relatively poor decisions.

For any activity, and this includes decision-making, we have to use some degree of Effort. Laban divided the application of Effort into four elements: Space, Force, Time and Flow and he linked these Effort elements to particular mental processes. Space was related to giving Attention, Force to determining Intention, and Time to commitment to decision-making. For example, to emphasise a desire would be seen in a movement of increasing pressure (Force), curiosity and inquisitiveness with a directing movement (Space), and so on.

In the years shortly before Laban's death, I was making movement observations, mostly in interviews with candidates seeking fairly senior positions in management, and I needed to find a coherent way to present my findings our clients. They needed firm advice on how well the candidates would cope in the situations they were interviewed for. When looked at from that point of view it became clear to me that although Laban had never regarded the Effort elements as parts of a process, what I was analysing was in fact the way in which people arrive at their decisions and that the need to take decisions large and small can be seen as what motivates us to act.

STAGE ONE – ATTENTION (SPACE)

First we must give attention to the issue. This may be by a small amount of attention equivalent to a glance, or it may be by a prolonged study of the issue, or it may be by anything ranging between the two spans of attention. We may want to study the matter and understand everything about its make-up, or we may assume that a glance has told us all we need to know. We may however prefer to take a wider view of the issue and explore the whole field in which it belongs.

STAGE TWO – INTENTION (FORCE)

Being aware that there is an issue to be dealt with, and having gathered what information we feel we need on it, we must then establish what our intention is in regard to it. What are our feelings on the matter; are we for or against, and what must we take into consideration? Is there a principle involved that we feel strongly about? Are there other matters or people to be taken into consideration? Do we wish to exert some authority here? Do we feel we could take a more philosophical attitude to it? To some people it will be important to weigh all these considerations in the balance, and to others such matters will be of less significance.

STAGE THREE – COMMITMENT (TIME)

After we have moved through these two stages, we can at last take action. There is no decision unless we go through the point of no return and this we may do in a quick clean instant: action. Or we may hold back for some time in a way which leaves other people unclear as to how we are going to act. Some people rush into decisions with barely a thought the moment their attention is drawn to something, others will agonise over taking a step even on a very trivial matter. Between the two there is every kind of possibility.

These three stages make up the decision-making model. No two people go through them in exactly the same way, some will give more Attention; some will rush virtually straight through to Commitment; most of us will at times fluctuate between the parts of the process, deciding we need more information after all, or that we must go back and work out our attitude again. Of course, this is influenced by circumstances – we may want to delay but circumstances prevent us from doing so and we thus have to act against our preference. We may find it impossible to choose between the various options and hesitate until there are no options remaining.

To recap: Laban described the Effort we put into movement as having four different qualities: Space, Force, Time and Flow. Flow he regarded as the relative degree of control in a movement, and this, as I will explain later, I believe should be dealt with separately. I have found it more meaningful to treat Flow as an element in its own right, rather than a separate category of the three Effort qualities.

Laban matched Attention with Space (Direct/Flexible) Effort; in other words a person going through the process of giving Attention to a subject would in the course of that process be using Effort on the continuum between Direct and Flexible. Similarly, he matched Intention with use of Force (Strong/Light) Effort, and Decision with the use of Time (Quick/Slow) Effort. I like to show them on a bi-polar basis, with each process having its extreme. The terms immediately below are those coined by Laban:

ATTENTION (SPACE)
Flexible..Direct

INTENTION (FORCE)
Light...Strong

COMMITMENT (TIME)
Slow..Quick

The terminology has since been developed to reflect more accurately the process being described as something which is on-going and changing.

ATTENTION (FOCUS)

Indirecting..Directing

INTENTION (PRESSURE)

Decreasing pressure...Increasing pressure

COMMITMENT (TIME)

Decelerating...Accelerating

The qualities of Effort have no particular attachment to geometric directions; for example, one can direct a glance or point a finger either up or down or sideways. They range between two extremes and at the extreme point of each polarity the movement would reach paralysis, a point rarely seen except in people under severe stress. Remembering that when we think of movement we are considering a constant state of flux, every movement has to be either reversed or stopped at some point or it will arrive at this paralysis. If we think of a continuum between, say, accelerating and decelerating, the reversal in speed of movement can take place at any part of the continuum.

These ranges of Effort can be summarised as:-

ATTENTION

Relates to what Laban regarded as the **Spatial**
qualities of movement **Indirecting/Directing** varies
between the polarities of a diffused focus
and wandering meander, to a more probing,
specific focus.

INTENTION

Relates to what Laban regarded as the **Force**
element of movement **Decreasing Pressure**
/Increasing Pressure varies between the polarities
of a light, releasing, fine-touch weakening, to a
stronger resistant pushing application.

COMMITMENT

Relates to what Laban regarded as the **TIME**
element of movement **Decelerating/Accelerating**
varies between slowing down, taking extra time,
dawdling to a speeding up, rushing through, setting
a fast pace.

The relativity should be taken into account. For example, "setting a fast pace" is not just one acceleration; there will be many, but the transitory "slowing down" (deceleration) will probably not go as far as "dawdling". Note that I have here added the fulcrum to show the neutral part of the range as the variations can take place at any part of the range between the two polarities, not necessarily passing through the neutral point. These variations of Effort can therefore be:

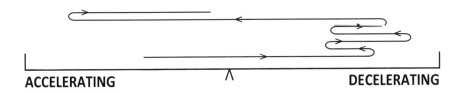

ACCELERATING   ∧   **DECELERATING**

If the process towards any polarity goes to the extreme there is paralysis, perhaps momentarily or it could be maintained for some time. For example, "dawdling" may decelerate to "dead stop".

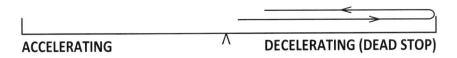

ACCELERATING   ∧   **DECELERATING (DEAD STOP)**

As we now know the Effort content of our movement is always related to the Shape content, and there needs to be a comparable list of Shape definitions. However, at this time (the mid 1950s) I was only just beginning to escape from the demand Laban imposed on me to confine my observations in Industry to Effort. It was approximately another five years before the Effort Shape Framework came together and this process will be described in Concept Three.

The relevance of these two aspects of decision making (1) that decision-making itself is a process and (2) that body movement is a process, occurred to me in the late 1950s when I was trying to sort out the constant stream of creative ideas fed to me by Laban. I came to the conclusion that the two processes could be matched and that when they do match in respect to movement which is Posture-Gesture merged (the subject of the second Concept) the person is manifesting his/her own pattern of decision-making preferences. When they do not match the person is probably under constraints preventing him or her from applying his/her preference and will experience some degree of stress. I found that when the matching processes do match on any decision-making occasion the decision-making is clearer than if they were mismatched, is carried through with minimum stress, has a positive influence on other people (which can be said to constitute leadership) and encourages good working relationships. Because it is based on process these benefits are cumulative.

I therefore built on the foundation Laban had laid down by demonstrating the connection of the three elements of Effort to the individual process of decision-making. At the same time I did include the qualities of Shape in my view of the decision-making process although Laban had never explicitly done this. Each element is necessary to the process, but they are not all given the same value by any one individual, and no two individuals give exactly the same value to any one part of the process. Just as in the decision-making process, so too in the movement related to it, some people will prefer to give more emphasis to one element and less to another.

The observer (the person making an analysis of another) does not seek to find out if the decision was this, that or the other, so much as to analyse the route taken to the decision. For example, if we say "Yes" or "No" it can be described as a decision but it may not be implemented (failure to follow through to Commitment). The individual may feel there is a need for further research affecting what is done (return to the Attention stage). Or there may be a lack of will to carry it through (an example of inadequate Intention).

Decision-making analysed in terms of movement is a continuing process between stages punctuated by different emphases.

I have never claimed that Movement Pattern Analysis tells us everything about a person's decision-making that we need to know. Carol-Lynne Moore explains the practical experience and research I built up over the years 1952 – 1970 as "Developing a Grounded Theory" (*Moore.* 2005. p38). She explains how, when a leader and his/her team members know each others Movement Pattern Analysis (MPA) profiles and work together with them, they combine and complement their strengths more effectively. There is also the important aspect, however, that a strong leader will choose a strategy which appeals to his/her decision-making style, and will reject any options which do not. Where such leaders have big responsibility some predictability is inevitable.

I regard my experience and research as having made a contribution to the history of decision-making. It may be argued that this decision-making model I pioneered has no great claim to fame because it is similar to many used in business and by the armed forces. Its distinctive merit, however, is that it relates directly to movement, movement which can be observed. Thought processes are reflected in movement processes, and our body movements are a window to our preferred way of decision-making. They are the indicator as to how we will deal with any given situation. Whether the decision is subsequently judged as right or wrong however, is in this context irrelevant. The movement analyst must only record what he/she sees. To the extent that they listen, they must do so non-judgementally.

I was impressed by a recently published book where a professor of neuro-science explained the importance of embodiment in relation to decision-making and he gave this example of someone he had observed: "the man rose from a seated position and moved forward". This is the closest to a movement description in such writings that I have ever read. I suggested to the author that he could have observed the person's movements as a sequence or as a process. For example, did the rising accelerate and then decelerate; did it increase in pressure or become light; was it precisely upwards or did it incline to right or left, or veer backwards a little, or incorporate some combination of these movements? With the transition forwards was there precisely directing movement or was there some degree of wriggle in it? Did the person also move to some degree downwards and sideways, either together or first one and then the other....? The author did not reply.

My hope is that advances in neuro-scientific research will lead to recognition that these questions need to be asked and answered. Computer modelling of the brain activity related to movement are already being created. Advances in understanding the intricate working of the human brain put together with advances in computer science can hopefully play a major role in providing an accurate recording of movement behaviour which is less reliant on the accuracy of the naked eye.

CONCEPT TWO

The isolation of the Posture-Gesture Merger (Integrated Movement) as containing the relatively enduring features of a person's movement as distinct from the transitory.

Posture – movement which is consistent throughout the body as a whole – an action involving continuous adjustment of every part of the body.

Gesture – movement confined to part or parts of the body – movement where some parts of the body are isolated from other parts in terms of movement.[1]

Posture-gesture merging occurs when a gesture merges into a movement of the body as a whole, or where a postural movement supports and is consistent with a gestural movement. There is a point in every person's behaviour at which posture and gesture merge and they will perform their posture-gesture merged movements regularly. It is something a person has to do in order to function satisfactorily. The manner of the merger of posture and gesture in a person's movement is the essential DNA of their behaviour. It is unique to the individual, it is what distinguishes one person from another. Furthermore, analysis of it reveals the preferred nature of their decision making. In using their posture-gesture merger the individual feels comfortable and at ease.

If the body and mind are regarded as two entities in negotiation with each other, then at this point there is harmony between the two, without one trying to dominate the other.

There are two examples I have often used to clarify what we mean by a posture-gesture merger (PGM) as opposed to movement of different parts of the body which are unmerged. First imagine a one-man band. The man has drumsticks on his elbows, cymbals tied to his knees, and a flute in his mouth. When he plays it can certainly be said that he is using all parts of his body simultaneously and that they may even be coordinated after a fashion. But if we ask what is actually happening, we find that the different parts of the body are not consistently contributing to the same processes of movement.

"The various gesture processes can only be maintained by extreme conscious control, and it is this deliberate forcing of bodily behaviour from its normal pattern that arouses both our uneasy admiration, and our sense of relief when the whirligig comes to a halt." (Lamb. 1979. pp 89-90)

A true posture-gesture merger (PGM) is therefore one with a smooth continuous momentum towards a single end. This is illustrated by my second example, which is to observe what happens when people wave goodbye to each other. Their physical behaviour almost always involves an arm action of raising, a hand action of waving and a lowering of the arm. If this is being done with any sincerity it will involve postural adjustment that will arise at different points in the process with different people. One person may start the rising arm gesture and merge it into a posture rising on the way upwards. Another person may confine the arm raising to gesture then involve posture with the first quick action of waving. There are many different possibilities for performing the wave, but to be sincere the early gestures all will flow into the single merger. If the farewell is confined to gesture alone it will most likely be felt as a rather meaningless action without any real emotion behind it. A predominance of such gestures in a person's behaviour gives it a mocking, insincere effect akin to a false smile or a routine handshake which expresses no emotion.

Think also of how to perform a manual task such as digging the garden. We have to take up a position in order to handle the spade, and if we do not make a postural adjustment to push it into the ground we will most likely feel discomfort and be in danger of injuring ourselves, as well as making a poor job of digging. It is generally the case that where gestures are not linked to postural adjustment the behaviour will look contrived, rather like "ham" acting. In a posture-gesture merger the Effort and Shape processes have to be consistent. For example, if the hand begins a process of increasing pressure, a merging into posture only happens if the whole body consistently "backs up" the hand action with a similar increase of pressure. If any part of the body opts out of this then a true posture movement is not made.

Each person has their own patterning of posture-gesture merger which they return to regularly throughout the day if circumstances permit. During the course of an interview of, say, an hour and a half, it has been found possible for a practitioner to observe and record the

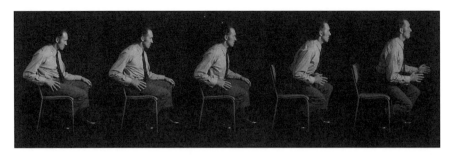

Fig. 2. A posture-gesture merger. *Starting from a retreating rest position the advancing hand gesture leads into a postural advancing. Note the convex curvature of the body (particularly the torso) in the forward back (sagittal) plane. (Excerpt from Top Team Planning)*[2]

components of the interviewee's posture-gesture merger while simply sitting in a room chatting. After the interview the movement analyst calculates from the notations taken, the ratio of components to each other, and matches the results of this against the decision-making model to define a profile of the person.

Identifying the posture-gesture merger is important because it provides understanding about what is relatively *enduring* in our behaviour as distinct from the many types of *transitory* change which everyone experiences during life to a greater or lesser degree. The individual's patterning of movement is generally formed during adolescence and into adulthood, after which only severe trauma will change it. Most of us have had the experience of meeting someone after a gap of many years, and although the person may have changed in many respects we almost always recognise them from their movement.

In other words we have a preferred decision-making sequence of movement, subject to only marginal change, throughout our adult life, and this is found in our posture-gesture merger. A person's movement will have many other features during their lives, whether fashionable or nervous, affected or unwittingly copied from someone, but these will only serve to overlay the intrinsic posture-gesture merger built up during earlier life experience.

Research into the validity of posture-gesture merger theory was carried out by Deborah du Nann Winter of Whitman College, Washington, and the results were published in the *Journal of Non Verbal Behaviour* in 1989. The research centred largely on my claim that the occurrence of the posture gesture merger is the result of sincere and not contrived behaviour. "Posture Gesture Mergers accompany verbal expressions that are truthful, relaxed, sincere, or authentic" she found. In conclusion she wrote, "Reliance on integrated movement leads us to look at that part of the person which is most alive, healthy and eager to act in the world".

More recently this research has been built on by Dr Mone Welsche who reported to a conference I attended in Germany in July 2010 on work she had done with adolescents. In this the incidence of PGM in two groups of native German speakers was calculated during an interview situation. One group was rated as being highly depressive and the other group as clinically non-noticeable. The research found that the highly depressive subjects produced significantly fewer PGMs than the control subjects, indicating that people with this mental disorder find difficulty in being engaged physically and psychologically in the on-going communication situation.

The research concluded:

"Building on the outcome of this study, a better understanding of movement behaviour of mentally ill as well as clinically non-noticeable female adolescents could be gained, which has the potential to enhance not only movement therapeutic treatment but also diagnostic procedures and clinical treatment in general."

Some movement study people have in the past offered courses purporting to change a person's PGM pattern. I think this is foolhardy because it cannot be achieved other than to a minor degree unless very extreme methods tantamount to brainwashing are used. Transformational change can appear attractive if we are dissatisfied with our existing situation. We can, for example, change our religion or become a born-again Christian, we can change temperamentally, becoming patient when we were formerly impatient; or we can stop being a banker and become a charity worker. These are changes which may or may not be transformational and which may remain permanent, but our movement pattern, derived from our PGM, will remain almost the same throughout our adult life.

I have run individual courses for which I designed sequences of movement compatible with the student's MPA profile. The students always enjoy doing this. Inculcating awareness of movement patterns which are individually distinct is in itself beneficial and the students can understand it in relation to their own life experience. Then I add a movement phrase to one of the sequences which is incompatible with their MPA profile. Immediately the student feels uncomfortable.

However mobile and athletic he or she may be, and however much we work to try and overcome the discomfort, we make no progress.[3]

With the codification of movement terms initiated by Laban we have the means to be specific. He taught me when observing movement not only to record phrases, but also to give some indication of the body parts in which I had observed the movement to happen. He himself often drew a picture of them. This is a good discipline and one that I have tried to continue throughout my career. I commend it to others; many observers are vague when asked in what parts of the body did they see the movement. It is as though the movement happened in thin air. Moreover, it is often a fixed position they have seen and not movement as a process of variation.

The terms Laban used for movement observation were Functional Action, Shadow Movement and Body Attitude. I found it impossible to define the difference between a Functional movement, for example wielding a hammer to knock in a nail, and expressive movement, presumably coming under the Shadow Movement category, perhaps threatening another person with a hammer. Laban selected examples that were clearly one or the other, but if "Functional" was to stand as a category then why, I asked myself, was there not an "Expressive" one?

Shadow Movement was defined as "small movements which flit across the surface of the body", these movements contained a message, an indication of mood perhaps. They were said to be "expressive", as indeed they can be, often dramatically so in some contexts. An eyebrow twitch was one he often quoted as an example. Actors find that reference to Shadow Movement can be helpful. An example is Bernard Hepton who attended lectures given by Laban and likes to relate that Laban told him, "I will teach you to act with your eyebrows". It then became confusing when the term Shadow Movement had to apply to bigger movement. I found it almost impossible to observe a twitch in terms of movement. And what happens when a small twitch stops being small and becomes something bigger?

I also had a problem with the term Body Attitude although it still frequently appears in the writings of Laban followers. It almost invariably has a static connection and often relates to "inner attitude". For me it is essential to use movement terms, and I am uncomfortable with "inner" and its note of mysticism. What is inner? We cannot see it. We might however interpret movement we *have* seen as having "inner" significance.

Part of the divergence must also lie in the way movement is being approached. Where it is being used to interpret mood, as in dance or theatre, has different requirements from my use of it in analysis. I struggled for years to sort all this out and eventually came to the conclusion that there are just two categories of movement, posture movement and gesture movement. At the same time I also recognised the overwhelming importance of the posture-gesture merger to the individual and that it would inevitably appear in their movement no matter what attempts they made to avoid it.

Endnotes

*(1) My book **Posture and Gesture** (1965) first gave these definitions. They can also be found in Chapter One of **Body Code** (1979) which treats this subject at length.*

*(2) **Top Team Planning** (1973) contains several similar illustrations pp 80-81*

*(3) An example of such a course is included in the DVD **Decision Making and Movement Pattern Analysis** which accompanies the book **"An Eye for Movement"** both by Dr Dick McCaw (Brechin Books Limited 2006).*

CONCEPT THREE

A systematic matching of Effort (Assertion) and Shape (Perspective)

Effort goes with Shape organically. We cannot move in making an Effort without an accompanying movement of Shaping. These are the two components of movement and they encompass all other ingredients. Some interpretations of my work make it appear that I invented the concept of Shape, but in fact Laban made it clear that this duality was the basis of his work with his definitions of Eukinetics (Effort) and Choreutics (Shape).

Fig. 3. A summary of the Framework when Effort and Shape are studied together

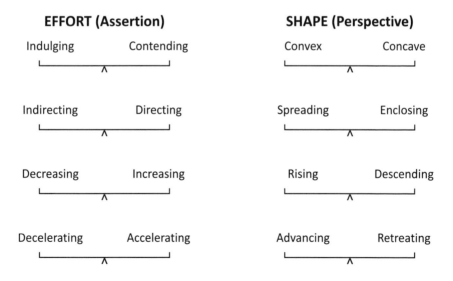

EFFORT (Assertion)		SHAPE (Perspective)	
Indulging	Contending	Convex	Concave
Indirecting	Directing	Spreading	Enclosing
Decreasing	Increasing	Rising	Descending
Decelerating	Accelerating	Advancing	Retreating

Fig.4. The brief definitions offered in Concept One are repeated together with the comparable Shape definitions.

EFFORT	SHAPE

ATTENTION

Focus	Horizontal
Indirecting/Directing	**Spreading/Enclosing**
Varies between the polarities of a probing, specific focus to a diffused focus.	Varies between the polarities of a closing, folding enwrapping, horizontally oriented movement to an open laterally reaching widening.

INTENTION

Pressure	Vertical
Decreasing/Increasing	**Rising/Descending**
Varies between the polarities of a strong, resistant pushing application of pressure to a lighter, releasing fine-touch weakening.	Varies between a sinking, hiding movement to a rising potentially levitational, vertically orientated elevation.

COMMITMENT

Time	Sagittal
Decelerating/Accelerating	**Advancing/Retreating**
Varies between the polarities of speeding up, rushing through setting a fast pace to a slowing down, taking extra time, dawdling.	Varies between the polarities of a retiring, withdrawing movement to an advancing, onward sagittally orientated progression.

31

The framework in Fig.2 was first published in *Posture and Gesture* in 1965 (p.62). Some of the terms have been changed for clarity over the years but the theory is the same and based entirely on what I learned from Laban. He also used the terms Indulging/Contending for Effort and Convex/Concave for Shape, which neatly describe the two groups of polarities. These are self explanatory but it should also be remembered that he preferred to use Gathering/Scattering for Shape, especially in contexts which included reference to both Effort and Shape.[1]

There are natural affinities between the various aspects of Effort and Shape and this is what is meant by "matching". The Indulging qualities of Effort combine more naturally with the Convex aspects of Shape, and the Contending qualities of Effort combine more naturally with the Concave aspects of Shape. For example, it is more natural to exert an increasing pressure of Effort in a downward than an upward direction (vertical plane of Shape); it is more natural to look around (Indirecting Effort) with an opening (spreading, horizontal plane of Shape) movement; and it is more natural to react to danger by darting with an accelerating Effort backwards (retreating Sagittal plane of Shape) away from it rather than towards it.

I added the terms Assertion to Effort and Perspective to Shape because they are synonymous and I found they were more readily understood in clarifying the decision-making concept, by the non-movement people with whom I have worked. Instead of the terms Laban always used to describe the "elements" of Effort – Space, Weight, Time and Flow – which I considered contained many ambiguities and encouraged people to philosophise about Space/Time and create confusion – I renamed them Focus, Pressure, and Time. As already mentioned, I have always regarded Flow as needing to be treated differently. (See Concept Five)

Laban's terms Direct/Flexible, Strong/Light and Quick/Slow invited for me images where there is no variation. I changed these to present participles to encourage awareness of process: Indirecting/Directing, Decreasing/Increasing, Decelerating/Accelerating. The use of see-saws was also introduced to emphasise that any bi-polar process must have an extreme when it either gets stuck or has to reverse. For example, increasing pressure leads to cramp if the process is not renewed by means of a transitory decreasing pressure to enable it to resume increasing pressure. Imagine a person with a desperate feeling about something on which he urgently needs to persuade a partner to take action   That person may keep increasing the pressure on the partner to an extent where any more pressure increase becomes impossible. This is the state which I call "cramp" and it probably looks ugly. All movement components have their limits where they either become paralysed or need to be reversed.

Horizontal, Vertical, Sagittal were the terms I decided on for the three matching processes of Shape. They were ridiculed by some reviewers of *Posture and Gesture* and unfortunately came to be referred to by some people as "shaping in the planes". I did not intend a two-dimensional connotation and a better choice might have been 'flattening' of the kinesphere (horizontal) or 'elongating' it (vertical) or 'propelling' it (sagittal), in order to give more sense to the movement.

The difference between Laban's work and my own lies in the way he treated Effort and Shape separately. In "Industry" I was to look at the Effort of the workers, and not to concern myself with Shape. Choreutics he saw as the expression of emotional or spiritual drives and more relevant to "Dance".

As the work we did in Industry progressed we were increasingly concerned with the whole personality of the workers we observed. To judge their suitability for particular types of work, their leadership qualities, or their ability to interact in a team, it was necessary to look not only at their Effort, but at such things as their demeanour among colleagues. It was this which brought me to the point shortly before his death when I told him I felt I should notate both Effort and Shape when making observations. He was slightly surprised but agreed that this was the way to proceed.

In this same context it was always my opinion that Laban's use of "Space" as an Effort term as well as in the subject "Space Harmony" created some confusion. Space harmony and all the movement scales associated with it had to do with shaping the kinesphere. Trying to make Shape appear as something different from Space so far as movement is concerned is limiting and has no theoretical basis.

Some people using Laban's name define Effort as *Attitude,* Shape as *Relationships*, and Space as *Pathway.* If we want to study attitude, relationships or pathways it is sounder to do so within the framework of Effort/Shape even though we give emphasis more to one particular aspect. There is also a danger of distortion or superficiality. For example, in making a pathway through space our shape does not stay the same; new sculptural forms are created and need to be taken into account, otherwise the pathway has no context of the body as a whole.

The framework I arrived at, in addition to enabling the matching of Effort and Shape, also puts Flow into what has proved a proper relationship with other Effort and Shape components. It encourages the perception of the relative incidence of all eight components and has led to the possibility of the Profile being shown as a series of lines with fulcrums, for example:

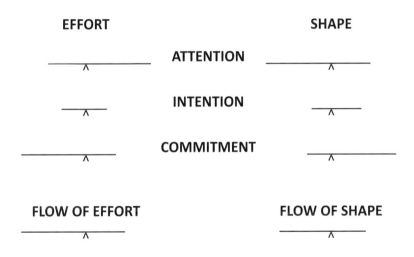

Fig. 5. The summary of an imaginary MPA showing in diagrammatic form the ratios of one component to another.

Dr Judith Kestenberg, who was my student then collaborator for many years, adopted this device and it is the basis of the Kestenberg Movement Profile. The Framework is also of course in the logical order of the decision-making process:

Shape (Perspective)		Effort (Assertion)
Horizontal	ATTENTION	Focus
Vertical	INTENTION	Pressure
Sagittal	COMMITMENT	Time

I trained Irmgard Bartenieff in it during the early 1960s, and she then set up the "Effort/Shape Department" of the Dance Notation Bureau in New York. In 1978 it became the Laban Institute of Movement Studies (LIMS) and diplomas were awarded in Effort/Shape. Many employers in the fields of dance and dance/movement therapy demanded the E/S qualification. Some still do, in Europe and other parts of the world as well as the U.S.

As with Concept One, I developed the Shape/ Effort Framework during the years following Laban's death when I was trying to organise what I had learned from him and fashion it into a framework that could be used in a practical way without any vague or discursive implications. I was compelled to give chapter and verse to the engineers and accountants employed by the management consultant F. C. Lawrence, Laban's collaborator, on how I observed movement. They and sometimes the clients wanted to know the detail of the notation record, how the record was analysed, and how it was translated into recommendations. Laban's charisma and guru-like pronouncements protected him from this sort of attack. For me, it provoked me to work towards the goal of a viable, clearly explainable framework.

Most of the terms movement people use have entered the lexicon, but it is essential to understand the concept of the duality of Effort/Shape, as did Irmgard Bartenieff in setting up LIMS (Laban Institute of Movement Study). Words could be changed, new words added, the design altered, but the concept has been proved valid, not only by MPA practitioners but also by Bartenieff, Kestenberg, and many others. We have barely scratched the surface of how it can be incorporated into the application of disciplined movement study in many fields, not only in decision-making. I like to think that the Effort/Shape framework, first published in 1965, will endure, and whilst I applaud any valuable development, I would very much regret any distortion of it.

The fact is we can never do Effort without Shaping and, if we emphasise the Shaping we still have to make an Effort. The two are a duality, inseparable from each other, and fundamental to balance. The complex of space harmonies, for example, (including all the scales worked out by Laban) cannot exclude Effort; I think it is good to perform them together using the Effort which goes most harmoniously with the Shaping.

Endnotes

(1) *See the recent translations from his writings in* **"The Laban Sourcebook"** *Ed. Dick McCaw (2011).*

CONCEPT
FOUR

The notion of affinities between Effort and Shape having significance for interaction.

Laban used to teach the dimensional scale in which the student had to align:

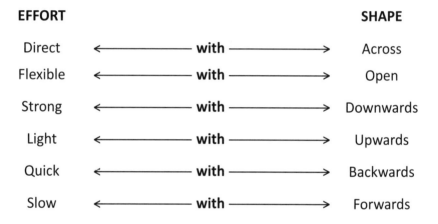

EFFORT		SHAPE
Direct	←——— with ———→	Across
Flexible	←——— with ———→	Open
Strong	←——— with ———→	Downwards
Light	←——— with ———→	Upwards
Quick	←——— with ———→	Backwards
Slow	←——— with ———→	Forwards

These associations were claimed to come "most easily" or "naturally". Over a period of years I abandoned the dimensional reference and saw them as significant in respect to the Effort and Shape processes. When people's matching or degree of affinity based on Laban's categorisation was clear from observation of their PGM movements, it seemed they related to other people differently from when there was mismatching. Reference was made to this discovery in *Posture and Gesture* (1965) and the three types of high-quality interactive environments they create, Communicative (Attention), Presentational (Intention) and Operational (Commitment), were described there as well as in *Management Behaviour* (1969).[1]

The belief is that where an individual's PGM shows affinities between Effort and Shape at each stage of the decision-making process, that person will tend to invite communication and collaboration from others. Where disaffinity exists at each stage the individual is less inviting of cooperation and may actually seek to be private. In group behaviour, the degree to which affinities and disaffinities exist at the various stages of the decision-making process between the people in a group will have an impact on how successfully they can work as a team.

My claim that our preferred way of decision-making can be understood from movement observation and analysis is epoch-making enough. This new claim, basically that movement harmony or lack of it influences how we relate to other people, may also be exceptional. Certainly thousands of clients have accepted my findings in this respect when I have explained to them how their movement patterning affects the reaction of other people to them. They have testified to the benefit of knowing this, and have provided a lot of corroboration.

It is generally accepted that some people are gregarious and like to be with other people a lot, while others prefer more to be loners. An example of a loner is the case of the entrepreneurial owner of a successful small company which was being acquired by a client of mine.

Fig. 6. The Framework of Management Initiative.

THE MOTIVATION TO INTERACT

The Decision Making Process in Relation to Others

ATTENTION

SHARING ATTENDNG:
Giving genuine attention to others listening to them and drawing them out. Inviting them to share in probing the existing situation and/or bringing in new aspects for attention. Sharing own process of investigating and exploring.

NEUTRAL ATTENDING:
Depending on the initiatives of other to catalyze interaction. Giving attention without any initiative either to bring others in or to keep them out of the attending process.

PRIVATE ATTENDING:
Investigating and exploring independently. Results are reported; others are kept out of the process of analysing and gathering information.

VERSATILE ATTENDING:
Switches sharing on and off; interdependent and independent.

INTENTION

SHARING INTENDING:
Making a positive demonstration, declaring intentions, influencing, persuading, emphasising, insisting, resisting and inviting others to do likewise; sharing own process of determining and evaluating.

NEUTRAL INTENDING:
Depending on the initiatives of others to catalyze interaction. Forming intention without any initiative either to bring others in or to keep them out of the intending process.

PRIVATE INTENDING:
Determining and evaluating independently; stating beliefs. Others are kept out of the process of forging and shaping resolve.

VERSATILE INTENDING:
Switches sharing on and off. Interdependent and independent.

COMMITTMENT

SHARING COMMITTING:
On the spot organising of people; creating a sense of urgency or slowing down the pace; spurring people on or delaying activity with alertness to implication of action and objectives; progressing the action and inviting others to do the same; sharing own process of timing and anticipating.

NEUTRAL COMMITTING:
Depending on the initiatives of other to catalyze interaction. Committing without initiative either to bring others in or to keep them out of the committing process.

PRIVATE COMMITTING: Timing and anticipating independently. Others are kept out of the process of timing and staging of action.

VERSATILE COMMITTING:
Switches sharing on and off. Interdependent and independent.

© Warren Lamb Associates

My client's strategy was to retain him (the owner) as CEO, integrate the company into his group, and accelerate its growth. When I made an MPA profile of the owner of the small company, it became apparent that he had lot of disaffinity in his Effort/Shape movement. Although he was respected for his personal life, paid his staff well, and was regarded as a business success, of the 26 people reporting directly to him none were in a close working relationship with him and all of them complained that they could not communicate with him. He had even set up a generous pension scheme without telling anyone. I advised my client that the strategy would fail if this man was retained as CEO. My client nevertheless went ahead with the acquisition saying that he liked the man and would help him build a team. It failed, and after two and a half years there was a costly reorganisation. During this period seven senior executives had been appointed and all had left saying that there was little communication with the CEO and they were denied essential information. This story is typical of how loners – people with a high need for privacy – behave.

Whatever systems are set up to facilitate communication, it has to be recognised that highly independent people – loners – will try to beat the system. However, it is extremely rare for anyone to be so much of a loner that he or she has no desire to interact in any of the Attention, Intention or Commitment stages of the decision-making process. By understanding in which stage the potential for interaction predominates, by however little, the potential for sharing can be developed.

For example, some people prefer to share their Attention but not their Intention and will create a primarily Communicative environment.

Others prefer to interact primarily by sharing their Intention but not their Attention, thus creating a Presentational environment. A group strong in sharing Attention will be mainly dependent on being in touch with other people when they do their attending and will try not to do it independently. The group strong in sharing Intention will like to have people around with whom they can express their Intentions and this can be a form of dependency; in other words, they cannot make up their minds unless they have support. But such people may be happy pursuing an investigatory project independently (like Sherlock Holmes) only becoming dependent when they have a result or opinion to report – "Elementary my dear Watson!" When people from each group have a meeting there can be serious misunderstanding unless their preferences are known. At the Commitment stage of the decision-making process highly competitive people often prefer to be independent when close to the "point of no return" and colleagues are made to feel pre-empted.

Many clients have taken this principle to heart and found it invaluable in building successful management teams. Gordon Taylor of Racal Instruments used to set up groups chosen according to their interaction profile so they would interact appropriately to what he wanted from them. For example:

for research - matching of Attention components

for problem solving - matching of Intention components

for drawing up a programme - matching of Commitment components.

One of the three different environments was thus created - the Communicative, the Presentational and the Operational according to the work that had to be done.[2] It is fruitful, I believe, for any organisation which works through committees to consider these points when issues have to be resolved. In 1965 I wrote in *Posture and Gesture* (p.153):

"In certain types of meeting, for example, we may feel that one type may meet the needs of the situation more appropriately than another. The following association perhaps has some validity:

A. Where a meeting is brought about for one person to seek the advice of the other the preferred type will be....... Communication.

B. Where the meeting is for one person to demonstrate to the other a new product and how to make it work.......Presentation.

C. Where the meeting is for both parties to co-operate in a task.......Operation.

This is not to suggest that two Communication types cannot for example, cooperate in doing a joint task. From the body movement point of view, however, they will certainly appear awkward, not very practical, poorly organised (unless an organised framework has been set up for them) and Operationally confused."

And in an article in *Management Today* in 1984 I suggested:

> "When behaviour contradicts strategy, there are basically two alternatives: change the strategy or change the people. The former is worth considering seriously, on the principle that, if you have a good chef, you open a restaurant. In other words, you build the strategy which is consistent with the strengths of the top management team. Alternatively, you appoint or develop top managers likely to act consistently with the strategy."[3]

In other words my advice would always be that it is unwise to expect people to behave continuously in ways which are against their natural behaviour, because this would lead to stress on the one hand and inefficiency on the other.

These principles have been applied not only in management consultancy for team-building and to improve the effectiveness of meetings, but also in many other fields including therapy and marriage counselling. When I taught matching/mismatching findings to Dr Kestenberg she immediately incorporated it into her work where it continues to be developed. There has also been development and new terms spearheaded by others into more divisions and I hope this will continue so long as it builds authentically from its base in movement analysis. I accepted the distinctions "Sharing" and "Private" which are consistent with my differentiation between terms "Interactive" than "Non-interactive", but the word "Sharing" does rather make me uncomfortable because of its popularity with "New Age" people who tend to translate it into sentimentality and a gushing expression of togetherness. "Versatile" and "Neutral" were added later to the "Framework to Interact". A convention has been adopted that if the analysis showed more than 50:50 in both "Sharing" and "Private" it should be called "Versatile" and if below 50:50, "Neutral".

I prefer a more practical understanding as applied in the hundreds of team building seminars I have run. Participants are helped to recognise how different they are in respect to the initiative they take to interact from the initiative they take to be independent. They also understand how it relates to their readiness to make themselves dependent on others as distinct from their preference for acting independently.

When it becomes more recognised how this aspect of movement can be studied in a disciplined way surely this concept will be admitted into the mainstream of some field of behavioural science. It is an aspect of how the Effort/Shape Framework can be applied to enable an understanding of relationships in a practical and disciplined way.

Endnotes

(1) *Dr Carol-Lynne Moore has given a further clear explanation of the effect of harmony or dissonance in each stage of the decision-making process in **Movement and Making Decisions** (2005).*

(2) *Experiments set up on similar lines were carried out by Tim Lamb for his Masters' thesis at Imperial College, London, and are described in **Beyond Dance: Laban's Legacy of Movement Analysis.***

(3) ***Motivation by Strategy,** Management Today, March 1984.*

CONCEPT
FIVE

The distinction of two types of Flow, Flow of Effort and Flow of Shape

The concept of Flow is most easily explained by imagining the amoeba-like movements of an infant before any social interaction has required it to discipline its actions. These are movements containing little Effort and creating little Shape: they spontaneously move from and towards the body with no apparent purpose or pattern. Flow links all other components of movement to give them balance, flexibility and grace. A lot of writings testify to Laban's categorisation of Flow as an Effort element; "Space, Weight, Time and Flow". For many Laban disciples this remains so. Effort components flow in the sense of being more Free or more controlled. A person allowing themselves to be blown along by the wind moves with total freedom and as they take control of their movement to avoid danger, their movement becomes increasingly Bound.

Flow of Effort therefore varies between:

Freeing_____Binding
                              ∧

It is my contribution that there is also a Flow of Shape. After years of intensive and often bewildering mentorship from Laban it became increasingly clear to me as I worked to crystallise the Effort/Shape Framework that there had to be an equivalent Flow on the Shape side. Of course there is, and I named the process Growing and Shrinking, that is growing and shrinking of our kinesphere, the 'space bubble' we carry around ourselves. People vary the size of their kinesphere according to how they feel about themselves and how they want to 'project' themselves. Laban had used such terms as "Pin", "Ball", "Wall" in connection with the shaping of the kinesphere but I felt these needed to be described in terms of movement – movement as a process of variation. In the case of Flow of Shape the variation therefore is between:

Growing_____Shrinking

When I returned to London from New York in 1953 having attended classes taught by Martha Graham I duly reported on my visit to Laban and he responded "She has no Flow; she is Bound". In fact, I came to the conclusion that there is a lot of Flow variation in her and her group's movement but it emphasised the Binding polarity rather than the Freeing polarity:

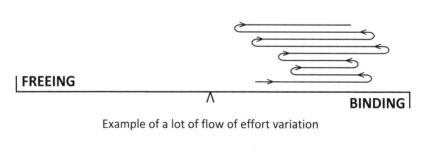

Example of a lot of flow of effort variation

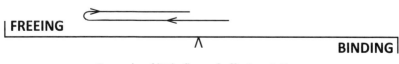

Example of little flow of effort variation

47

Accordingly, she could be doing more Flow variation than someone in whom Flow was primarily Freeing but who did not do many variations. If Martha Graham's Flow had shown little variation, or if it had been relatively neutralised (with slight variation around a mid-point between the polarities), she would never have achieved her immense appeal.

Seeing the two Flows in relation to each other and in relation to the other Effort and Shape components has proved immensely fertile. The terms have caught on and probably many people do not know that they were developed by me from Laban's teaching. Some of the definitions I now hear of what constitutes Flow of Shape surprise me. Nevertheless, other outcomes from studying Flow of Shape in its own right have made a very valuable contribution to movement study. Two of these are dealt with as separate issues in Concepts Six and Seven, both of which are concerned with the retention of Flow into adulthood.

To recap, Flow of Effort is described as operating on a continuum between Freeing and Binding, and Flow of Shape as operating on a continuum between Growing and Shrinking. We have also discussed in Concept Three the affinities between Assertion in Effort and Perspective in Shape, where we said that the natural affinity is between Indulging Effort and Concave Shape, and between Contending Effort with Convex Shape.

To these affinities we can now add the affinity between:

EFFORT

Freeing		Binding
Indulging		Contending
Indirecting	FOCUS	Directing
Decreasing	PRESSURE	Increasing
Decelerating	TIME	Accelerating

SHAPE

Growing		Shrinking
Convex		Concave
Spreading	HORIZONTAL	Enclosing
Rising	VERTICAL	Descending
Advancing	SAGITTAL	Retreating

Fig. 7. The Affinities of Flow of Effort and Flow of Shape

The person allowing themselves to be blown along by the wind (Fig 8) will naturally combine Freeing Flow of Effort with the Indulging elements of Effort until they decide enough is enough and they control their movement with the use of Binding Flow of Effort combined with the Contending elements of Effort. Similarly a person walking along a narrow path (Fig 9) surrounded by prickly bushes will combine their Binding Flow of Effort with Contending elements of Effort to carefully guide themselves between the branches. The use of Effort therefore determines how we use the environment to suit our own ends.

Fig. 8. A girl blown by the wind- Freeing Flow of Effort

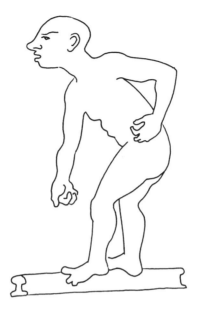

Fig. 9. A man walking on a railway line – Binding Flow of Effort

The use of Shape is more to do with how we feel about ourselves in relation to our environment. If we are nervous or ashamed we are inclined to make ourselves smaller and humbler, if we are confident and ebullient we will make ourselves bigger, we extend instead of shrinking our kinesphere. In *Beyond Dance* Eden Davies relates a story from my records which demonstrates the effectiveness of using Growing Flow of Shape.

"A General Manager of a subsidiary company, Mr A, commented that he greatly respected his Group Chief Executive, Mr X, for his handling of a group of people. 'When Mr X is talking to a group of people I have observed him to take a step or two backwards to preserve a distance between himself and the group and this seems to set him apart as a leader. However, when I try to do the same thing people follow me'. Actually Mr X was Growing as he stepped back giving himself a bigger kinesphere and thus maintaining the same contact with his audience. Mr A did not have the capacity to Grow his kinesphere and his group tried to follow him to maintain contact."(p.50)

The way in which we use Flow is therefore critical to our effectiveness. No matter how Directing we may be in our Effort to find the reason for something, if this is combined with Freeing Flow of Effort it will have less impact and may even look more playful rather than serious. Similarly a speaker proclaiming on the greater good to be achieved by his recommendations will hardly drive his message home if he combines his grand ideas with Shrinking Flow of Shape.

This is not to say that there are never occasions when the use of the disaffinity may not be effective. If we take the example of a man or woman walking onto a podium to speak at a conference they will probably enter the stage with Growing Flow of Shape to show their self-confidence, and perhaps combine this with spreading their arms in greeting to the audience (Convex Shaping). Supposing, however, they instead make an Enclosing movement, bringing their arms across to straighten a tie, clasp a folder, or pull the sides of their jacket together, while still maintaining the Growing Flow of Shape. The disaffinity in this case might be more appropriate to the situation depending on the relationship of the speaker to the audience and the nature of the occasion. There will be a sense of "I am here for a serious purpose and I'm one of you" rather than "I am your great and popular leader".

On the subject of disaffinity, it has been my experience to notice in the many years I have made profiles, that there is a *tendency* for men and women to make different combinations of Flow with Shape and Effort. Put at its broadest the tendency is for women to combine Freeing Flow of Effort with the Contending elements of Effort (disaffinity), while men combine the Freeing Flow of Effort with the Indulging elements of Effort (affinity). Both would also make the differing combinations with Binding Flow of Effort. In the case of Shape women tend to make the affined combinations of Flow of Shape and Shape elements, whereas men make the disaffined combinations.

Fig. 10. A woman holding a baby uses Enclosing Shape together with Shrinking Flow of Shape.

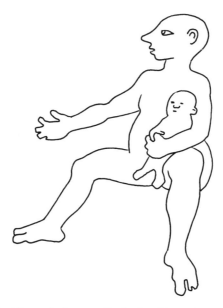

Fig. 11. A man holding a baby uses Enclosing Shape to protect the baby but combines this with Growing Flow of Shape.

This theory has yet to be researched, and it is one that could open a can of worms at a time when gender issues can be so contentious. There is no clear movement patterning we can call "feminine" in that it is the preserve only of women, and there is no clear movement pattern which we can call "masculine" which is only performed by men. We all carry some degree of the opposite sex in us. All one can say is that nature and/or nurture have somehow produced some movement which would be regarded as feminine which is found mostly in women, and other movement which is regarded as masculine which is found mostly in men. It is my belief that Effort is more clearly visible in male movement and Shape is more clearly visible in female movement, because of the affinities made with the Flow of Effort and Flow of Shape. Neither can be described as better or worse than the other, and both can achieve the same results, but they will do so by quite different routes. Should it be proven by research that there is this distinction between the way men and women prefer to use their movement, a closer study of the implication of this could surely lead to a greater understanding of the problems underlying gender issues.

**CONCEPT
SIX**

The Framework which divides the three-stage Decision-Making Process into six basic actions and three interactions together with three overall factors (Identifying, Dynamism and Adaptability)

Identifying is a quality resulting from the degree of retention of Flow in adult behaviour. As a person matures from childhood the layers of Effort and Shape in their movement increase and the level of Flow diminishes. In some people a high degree of Flow is lost and in others the Flow retention is high. Where the Flow retention is high movement is more fluid, more easily adjusted to any given situation. The person can change their behaviour to suit the circumstances they find themselves in, perhaps even unconsciously; they will naturally "join in". Where there is this high Flow content in their behaviour there is the danger they will be indiscriminate in whom they decide to ally with, whereas a lower retention of Flow might suggest that more discernment will be used.[1]

Some companies develop a corporate culture which predominantly encourages Identifying among their staff, whilst others might have a culture encouraging a more individual and private competitiveness. There was a good example in the 1980's of contrasting business cultures within IBM and Hewlett Packard, two comparable IT corporations with which I was familiar.

Fig. 12. The framework for Management Initiative.

THE MOTIVATION TO ACT

The Decision Making Process in Action

ATTENTION

INVESTIGATING: Making the effort to probe, scan and classify information within a prescribed area.
Outcome: Systematic research, establishing method and defining standards.

EXPLORING: Gaining perspective by perceiving the scope available, uncovering, encompassing and being receptive to information from many areas.
Outcome: Creative possibilities, discovering alternatives.

INTENTION

DETERMINING: Making the effort to affirm purpose, build resolve, forge conviction, justify intent.
Outcome: Persisting against difficult odds, resistance to pressure.

EVALUATING: Gaining perspective by perceiving relative importance, weighing up the immediate needs and sizing up the issues.
Outcome: Clarity of intention, crystallising issues, realism.

COMMITMENT

TIMING: Making the effort to pace implementation, to adjust the moment by moment timing of action.
Outcome: Alertness to tactics and time priorities for opportune implementation.

ANTICIPATING: Gaining perspective by perceiving the developing stages of action and foreseeing the consequences of each stage.
Outcome: Setting goals, measuring progress and up-dating plans.

OVERALL FACTORS
DYNAMISM: The number of novel or non-routine cycles of decision-making the manager will simultaneously initiate and continue.

ADAPTABILITY: Willingness to alter basic attitudes to fit in with changed situations.

IDENTIFYING: The readiness to respond, participate and become involved in the action.

© Warren Lamb Associates

IBM employees showed primarily a high gain of Effort/Shape and a high loss of Flow of Effort and Flow of Shape. The corporation was known by its preference for formal procedures and working relationships. Employees preferred to shut themselves in their offices in order to get most of their work done and maintained this sense of detachment and formality at department meetings. One typical rule at IBM was that all male employees should wear long socks so as not to expose bare skin.

Such an order would never have been issued from within the contrasting culture of Hewlett Packard, whose employees showed primarily high retention of Flow of Effort and Flow of Shape, together with high gain of Effort/Shape. The company promoted open plan offices and were known for their culture of "management by walking around". Executives, especially managers, had to walk around several times a day visiting colleagues who in turn had to welcome them, whatever they were doing. A typical rule was that no-one could have an office unless they occupied one which was in the building before the company moved in, and if they had such an office they were not allowed to close the door. Only lawyers were excused from this rule. Such contrasting cultures mostly attract employees who are suited to the culture otherwise they do not stay long. Or they do things, as they did at Hewlett Packard, like putting plants and decorations around their desks to create a semblance of an office.

Dynamism has proved to be an important item with my clients; it is derived from Laban's concept of the "loading" of movement, i.e. the amount of variation occurring in proportion to the number of actions. Where a person puts more than one Effort quality and/or more than one Shape process into a posture-gesture merged movement their movement is more complex and has a greater intensity in order to maintain balance. They are people capable of handling several projects at once, whereas a person of low dynamism will usually want to finish one thing before starting another. In management teams people with lower dynamism will often feel that their colleagues with high dynamism "take on too much".

A dynamic person also has more potential for leadership which is an attractive quality if it is used with discrimination and sensitivity. It should never be assumed that a high degree of dynamism necessarily goes hand in hand with a high IQ, any more than a person with a high IQ can be assumed to have dynamism and leadership qualities.

Adaptability is now omitted from the Framework because it is interpreted from the Profile itself and not directly from the movement observation and analysis. In other words it is a quality only deduced from the MPA profile once it has been completed. I have included it in the Overall Factors because I have found it to be a useful concept to use in discussions with clients, particularly when managing change in their organisations.

To adapt usually means to change. Many management consultants tell their clients they have to change without being able to say from what to what. I found that those managers or consultants who wanted to take the initiative to introduce change had an MPA profile in which their predominant preference was for the Attention Stage. In contrast a manager whose profile showed preference for the Commitment Stage often thought he or she was introducing change simply by cutting targets. It is necessary to know the relative preference between the stages in the decision-making process (described in Concept 4) to know the person's motivation for introducing change. It is also important to bear in mind that people who are highly adaptable may be in danger of instituting change for its own sake. Not only at corporate level but also at a national level, it is too easy for governments to confuse effective government with target-setting without implementing the means to ensure that management standards are maintained while the targets are being met.

If people work together effectively as a team they may truly achieve adaptation. It has been found that where members of a team are each familiar with the others' MPA profiles, they can more easily discuss whose initiative would be foremost in accomplishing change or adaptation.

These brief explanations of **Identifying, Dynamism and Adaptability** only scratch the surface of what the Effort/Shape framework has contributed to disciplined study. I believe that when more sophisticated technology is used for movement observation and the analysis process its importance in The Seven Creative Concepts will be substantiated. Meanwhile the inclusion of these three overall factors in the Framework of Management Action has in thousands of cases contributed to an improved understanding and a more positive outcome.

"The Framework of Management Initiative: The Motivation to Act" is originally a translation of the Effort/Shape framework into terms which my clients could relate to their own experience and as such it has been very successful. On the other hand, unfortunately, it has opened the way to these terms often being used divorced from any appreciation of the movement observation from which they were derived. Having a "Framework of Management Action" as it is called, labelling the decision-making process in terms of Attention – Intention – Commitment, with their component parts such as Investigating, Exploring etc., is no great discovery. I have always recognised that frameworks in similar terms abound and are used for their own purposes. What makes this Framework special is its derivation from posture-gesture merged movement and MPA practitioners believe that it should only be used with this understanding.

The actual terms of the Framework have stood up remarkably well. I used "Deciding" initially so as not to use the movement term "Timing" but it was sensibly replaced because, of course, the whole process is "Deciding". Otherwise I changed "Disciplining" into "Determining" and reluctantly agreed to change "Confronting" into "Evaluating". No more changes have been made for over thirty years and to make any more now would just be pedantic.

As someone who has fought for getting the Effort/Shape framework understood in true terms of movement, I would like to think it will always be appreciated as process and flux, and as a duality which can be sub-divided but not tampered with.

Endnotes

*(1) **Moore** (2005) p.91*

CONCEPT
SEVEN

The recognition that Flow (of Effort and Shape) diminishes during childhood growth while the Effort and Shaping movement of the three stages of the Decision-Making Process are being developed.

This concept arises from my observation that the movement of an infant contains little visible Effort or Shape content, but is mostly Flow, freeing and binding, growing and shrinking without any control. As the baby matures Effort and Shape components are added to its movement, and the Flow content diminishes. I realised that the ratio between gain of Effort/Shape to "loss" or "expense" of Flow could be estimated. I preferred to refer to "expense" rather than "loss", on the basis that Flow could be regarded as a currency it is necessary to spend in order to achieve adulthood.

Using this Flow expense/Shape, Effort gain ratio it is possible to place adults in four relative groupings. Those below are adapted from the four possible permutations listed in *Posture and Gesture.*

1. **High Shape/Effort gain and high Flow expense** - these people will be physically very competent in organising their own lives and will be personally very efficient as adults. They will, however, often be felt by others to be rather aloof and, for example, would not tend to be naturally good with children.

2. **Low Shape/Effort gain and high Flow expense** – these people will be neither physically efficient as adults nor able to engage with children. They will probably be characterised as awkward.

3. **Low Shape/Effort gain and low Flow expense** – these people remain childish which is a less desirable state than the ability to be *childlike*. They retain a physical behaviour age far below their actual age and appear immature.

4. **High Shape/Effort gain and low Flow loss** – to me this represents a mature Shape/Effort development together with an ability to respond easily to activity of others in the environment. These are the people who are confident enough to allow a spontaneity and sense of fun in their physical behaviour; they demonstrate a natural ease and facility, and are competent at the same time.

In the 1950s I conducted research into the movement of newborn infants up to the age of 10 years with Dr Judith Kestenberg . Her group of psychiatrists carried the research through to the age of 22 with three of the subjects. The results of this work was written up in *Children and Parents* (1978) and confirms the theory that Flow diminishes as the Effort and Shape components grow.

The discovery (if that is what it is) may have prime potential in the field of education. I have always felt that for children to become adult having retained a relatively high degree of Flow was a good thing. I thought it enabled them to participate in activities with children in a spontaneous way while adults who had retained relatively little Flow variation appeared to be aloof. Observations showed that children are more responsive to the participative adults than to aloof ones. This is the case even though aloof people may want to participate with children in the sense of giving them attention, offering them presents, trying to play with them, and perhaps genuinely expressing feeling for them.

My professional handling of the MPA Profile, however, demanded that there is never any good or bad, per se, about any one person's Profile. Over the past few years I have come to believe that for children to become adult with low retention of Flow is not necessarily undesirable – there are other factors. Why is it bad for people to have an aloof manner if it suits them? It may have advantages over a participative manner in some contexts. How it blends with their interaction preference is the important factor.

And when do we become adult? It is not long since the ages of 12 to 13 were regarded as the advent of adulthood and this is still the case in many cultures. In the West where adolescence tends to be more protracted, it may be that an understanding of the "gain/expense" ratio as well as the emerging preferences for Interaction and the Effort/Shape components, could be a major contribution to the education of young people. A practical knowledge of their physical development in movement terms during those confusing years would be a great advantage. Adolescence is recognised as a critical time for young people to sort themselves out, particularly in personal relationships and in respect to range of movement. Unhappy experiences at this time of life can have the effect of reducing a person's range.

Movement education is still in its infancy and there is little understanding of how the development of a range of movement should be taught. Sports training is highly scientific and sophisticated but does not necessarily develop range of movement; often the highly specialised training required to excel in some sports does exactly the opposite. In the Laban Lecture of 1986 I made this prediction: "For children to grow up intellectually brilliant but obtuse in the way they move their bodies will be regarded with as much disdain or compassion as illiteracy is currently viewed". What I would like, when Flow becomes better understood by educators, is for my concept of the Effort/Shape/Flow "gain expense" ratio to become a topic of debate.

CONCLUSION

Laban taught that movement is the common denominator of all activity. To me this was inspirational. It was not just a "discovery" but a statement of a truth so basic and yet so seldom recognised. Throughout my career I have stressed this point to my students. Everything we do requires movement, even breathing, and movement is a constant state of flux. Laban also taught that we arrive at adulthood with our distinctive movement pattern – what I have called our posture-gesture merging - that we use many times a day, and which is important to our sense of well-being.

Since movement is so fundamental to our lives and our individuality, I believe, as Laban did, that everyone should have the opportunity to learn the basic principles of movement. They should be taught from an early age so that each person has the chance to grow up with more understanding and therefore more command over their own physical and mental health. At the Art of Movement Studio we were trained in *movement* for three years, after which we could choose how we would use our training, whether that would be in dance, the theatre, in therapy, in industry or whatever. The essential was to thoroughly understand movement first.

When Laban began his work in industry with Lawrence they introduced the notion of Industrial Rhythm to replace the discredited ideas of Time and Motion Study. The theories, (which included what they called Lilt in Labour for the work women did in factories during the war) were based on the belief that at work, as at play, movement should have dignity and be joyful. Where stress is put on the body they said it should be neutralised by compensatory exercises, and stress would not necessarily be caused by heavy or hard work; it could also be caused by work as light as repetitively putting wrappers on Mars Bars. It was proved that such principles as this benefitted output, even when workers were taken away from the production lines for short intervals. Work was a more enjoyable experience and there was less absenteeism.

The theories they applied then are just as valid today. Production lines may be mostly a thing of the past but they have been replaced by banks of computer screens and these set up their own raft of problems. Working conditions have changed, in many cases out of all recognition and on the whole people are required to do less movement for longer periods of time, and yet "stress" has replaced "back-ache" as the most common cause of long-term absenteeism.

A great many people, appreciating the dangers of being physically inactive, balance this with regular exercise of some sort. This desire to maintain a level of fitness would have added value if there was a wider understanding of movement; not only the individual but society as a whole would benefit.

My use of Laban's theories of movement has been primarily in the category he devised called "Industry"; this I translated into "Management" in that I worked almost exclusively with senior executives. Apart from this I have also been involved in a wide range of fields.   I have worked in therapy, with psychiatric patients, with artists, in individual career management and in the theatre. At the same time I have kept in touch with my fellow students from the Art of Movement Studio who mostly chose to spend their careers in the world of dance, and they, like me, have always worked towards an ever deeper understanding of Laban's theories. A common meeting ground has been the Laban Guild, (I was President in the 1980s). My particular contribution to Laban-based movement study has been in pioneering Movement Pattern Analysis, and the essential basis of this is the Effort/Shape framework. The Effort/Shape framework has, however, proved to have a wider application to many other areas of movement study, in particular to Dance Therapy.

People working in any aspect of Laban Studies, whether students, researchers or practitioners, range from rigorously scholarly academics to the indifferently superficial who use Laban's name with little or no knowledge of his teachings. Laban's appeal has continued for more than 50 years since his death and is probably expanding while at the same time becoming dispersed and fragmented. There is no one organisation exercising control or guidance at all comparable, for example, to the Jungian Centres which are in many parts of the world. Two or three generations of Laban students exist but only a few people who actually worked with Laban are still alive. Some of Laban's ideas have been absorbed into various bodies of knowledge without present day students being aware of their derivation from Laban, notably in the theatre. In some fields unfortunately his name is used to enhance work little connected to his teachings. All this is perhaps inevitable given the profusion of ideas that is his legacy, and we must concentrate on applauding the richness of his contribution to knowledge, and focus on the wealth of what is good that is done in his name.

A large part of the danger is that Laban did not create a system and repeatedly said he did not want to. Accordingly, anyone can create new "Laban" terms (as I have done) and they have proliferated. If their use encourages people to become more aware of how their bodies move it is a good thing. It does, however, mean that there is confusion over how Laban's creative vision can be promoted for the benefit of humanity. For example, it is only in recent years that a coherent understanding has begun to emerge about Laban's discoveries with regard to movement harmony, the subject of *"The Harmonic Structure of Movement, Music, and Dance According to Rudolf Laban"* by Carol-Lynne Moore.

In this immensely broad and far-reaching range of Laban's work where do Movement Pattern Analysts fit in? It is certainly not just in "Industry" as Laban saw it and not just as the promoters of a form of personality assessment. We have developed, from Laban's teachings, a new discipline of movement observation and analysis. In other words it is not just a technique – it is a discipline which can stand as a subject in its own right. At the heart of Movement Pattern Analysis there are two clear statements of principle I have felt the need – in recent years more than ever – to insist upon:

1. That Effort/Shape is a duality

2. That movement is a process of variation

It is important to stress that movement terms cannot be used to describe fixed images. And while we can choose to observe the flux of Effort and Shape separately it has to be recognised that every Effort is Shaped in some way, and every act of Shaping requires Effort. These two principles, called by Laban Eukinetics and Choreutics, form the core of Laban's teaching and the framework I have developed encapsulates them.

We must always be alert, however, to a recent trend to use Laban's name when practising static forms of movement (almost a contradiction in terms) compared to the dynamic forms encouraged by Laban himself. Practitioners are sometimes using movement terms to describe non-movement in classes and workshops which use a predominance of static, dimensionally oriented movement designed to make it easy to maintain balance. In therapy a lot of work is done on the floor, frequently there is much more talking than moving, and a lot of use of slow motion; observations of fixed positions are described using movement terms; reference is made to "integrated" movement when in fact it consists of movement of part of the body only, what I call "gesture".

One illustration is the way "Bartenieff Fundamentals" is now taught. As already mentioned Irmgard Bartenieff was a student of Rudolf Laban in Germany and thoroughly absorbed his movement philosophy. After his death she took Effort/Shape courses with me before starting the Laban Institute of Movement Studies in New York. Her teaching and therapy work had the dynamic element consistent with Laban's teachings. It was a distinctive element which differentiated her "Fundamentals" technique from, for example, yoga and techniques such as Alexander and Feldenkrais. Now, sadly, this distinctive element is less evident.

Other therapies and styles of training have their place in the overall picture and make a valuable contribution to health and physical development in their own particular way. The important point for me is that they should not be linked to the name of Laban because this can only lead to a confusion of ideas in which his achievement is diminished.

"Dynamism" in movement, for example, should not be interpreted as consisting of intensive activity or of the remarkable acrobatics that athletes and dancers often exhibit. What it does consist of is second nature to students who worked with Laban himself. Have his first generation students failed to pass it on? Fortunately there are some exceptions and, hopefully, these people will keep this distinctive dynamic movement element alive as the true core of Laban's teaching.

Looking many years ahead I like to imagine that Movement will one day be taught in schools as a subject in its own right, and in a fashion appropriate to each age group right up to late teens. I like to think it will be taught separately from the arts, dance, physical education or sports, but it clearly would be helpful to those and other activities, just as the teaching of basic skills in reading, writing and arithmetic are also a common denominator to all aspects of learning. Laban certainly wanted Movement to be taught as a subject in its own right. I believe this will come about although it will take longer than the lifetime left to me. The present discussions on the place of physical activity in the National Curriculum may yield some results. If dance were to be included this would hopefully open the way for the principles of movement to have a place in the syllabus. On the subject of education it is very welcome news that in autumn 2012 a new post-graduate course is to be opened in Columbia College, Chicago. Called

Movement Pattern Analysis Consultant Certificate, it will run from September through to July.[1]

But in everything I do or say about Laban I try to keep his vision alive and my contribution is primarily the seven creative concepts. For movement study to progress it must be based on clear definitions and sound principles. Throughout my career my greatest problem has been to guard against superficial popularisation of the basic tenets. To have validity the decision-making process must be analysed only in terms of movement; the qualities of Effort and Shape are never fixed but are in a constant state of flux, where labelling of the various degrees is impossible; integrated movement only occurs when the whole body is involved. My intention is that this booklet will serve as a useful touchstone for current and future students of movement.

Endnotes

(1) *Columbia College, Chicago is launching the first ever graduate certificate in Movement Pattern Analysis. This is a year-long 13 credit program starting in summer 2012. It consists of five courses: Introduction to Laban Movement Analysis. Movement Pattern Analysis I, Entrepreneurship, Movement Pattern Analysis II, and Team-Building. For more information go to the following link: http://www.colum.edu/Academics/DMTC*

ACKNOWLEDGEMENTS

Several people have helped and encouraged us with this publication. Warren's daughter Imogen, a journalist, read the first draft and gave us valuable advice on setting the tone and direction of the book. James McBride, Carol Lynne-Moore and Mone Welche, all Movement Pattern Analysts, have each brought their professional experience to bear at later stages of its production. Dick McCaw, Senior Lecturer in Movement and Drama at Goldsmiths and Royal Holloway Colleges, University of London, and Ann Nugent, Senior Lecturer in Dance at the University of Chichester, both have advised on technical aspects of publication. We are grateful to all of them and to others who have helped in this project.

For myself, it has been a true pleasure to collaborate with Warren on this important statement of his basic concepts of Movement Pattern Analysis. I first met and worked for Warren in 1966, a year after the publication of his ground-breaking Posture and Gesture. His passionate fascination with movement was contagious then and remains undiminished. He has never suggested it is easy to become an accurate observer of movement, but his enthusiasm has inspired so many people to learn about movement. The seven concepts presented here form the basis of Warren Lamb's unique approach to human movement and decision-making, and are a distillation of his life's work.

Eden Davies.

BIBLIOGRAPHY

Amigi, Loman, Lewis & Sossin. *(1999) The Meaning of Movement: Development and Clinical Perspectives of the Kestenberg Movement Profile.* London, Gordon and Breach.

Davies, Eden (2006) *Beyond Dance: Laban's Legacy of Movement Analysis.* London, Routledge.

Davies, Eden. (20002) *Men and Women are so Different.* Movement and Dance Vol 21/3 & 21/4, 2002. Also available from Brechin Books Ltd.

Kestenberg Judith. (1975) *Children and Parents, Psychoanalytical Studies in Development.* New York, Jason Aranson.

Lamb, Warren. (1965). *Posture and Gesture: An Introduction to the Study of Physical Behaviour.* London, Gerald Duckworth & Co. Ltd. Now available from Brechin Books.

Lamb, Warren & Turner, David, (1969) *Management Behaviour.* London, Gerald Duckworth & Co.

Lamb, Warren & Watson, Elizabeth Watson. (1979) *Body Code: The Meaning in Movement.* London, Routledge & Kegan Paul.

Longstaff, Jeffrey. *Continuous Flux in the Flow of Effort and Shape.* (2008) in Movement and Dance Vol27 No 4 Winter 2008. A version of this article is also available from Brechin Books Ltd.

McCaw, Dick (2006) *Decision Making and Movement Pattern Analysis.* DVD ROM, London, Brechin Books.

McCaw, Dick. (2006) *An Eye for Movement: Warren Lamb's Career in Movement Analysis*. London, Brechin Books.

McCaw, Dick. (2011). *The Laban Sourcebook.* London, Routledge.

Moore, Carol-Lynne. (1982). *Executives in Action, A Guide to Balanced Decision-Making in Management.* London, Pitman.

Moore, Carol-Lynne. (2005). *Movement and Making Decisions: The Body-Mind Connection in the Workplace.* Dance & Movement Press, New York

Moore, Carol-Lynne. (2009). *The Harmonic Structure of Movement, Music and Dance According to Rudolf Laban: An Examination of his Unpublished Writings and Drawings.* Lampeter, The Edward Mellen Press.

Moore, Carol-Lynne & Kaoru Yamamoto (2011) *Beyond Words: Movement Observation and Analysis.* 2nd Edition. Routledge.

Ramsden, Pamela. (1973). *Top Team Planning, A Study of the Power of Individual Motivation in Management.* London, Cassell Associated Business Programmes.

INDEX